TIME FOR KIDS READERS

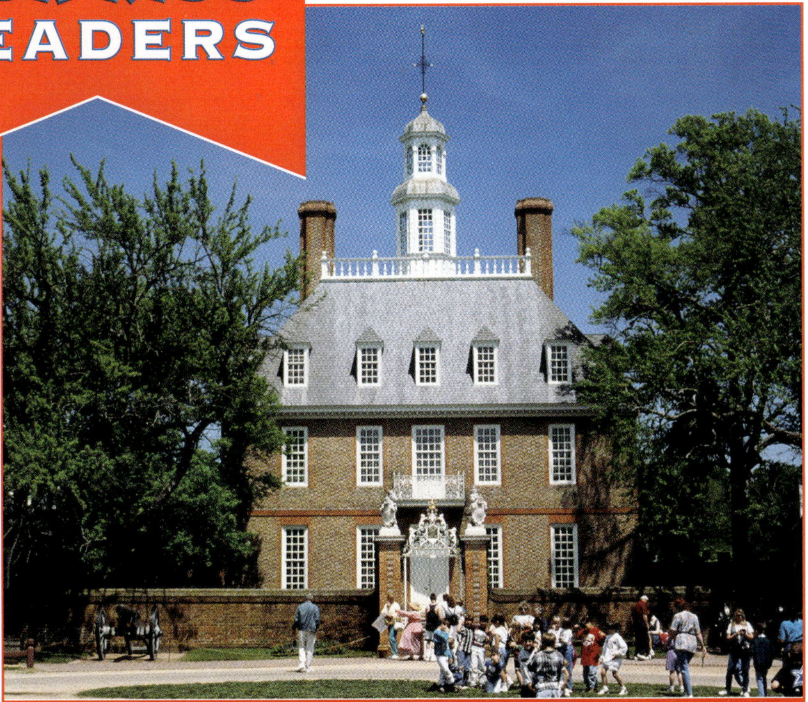

the restoration of Williamsburg

by Lisa Kline

Orlando   Austin   Chicago   New York   Toronto   London   San Diego

Visit *The Learning Site!*
www.harcourtschool.com

The start of a dream coming true: William Goodwin (left) and John D. Rockefeller, Jr., meet at Williamsburg in 1926.

In 1926, an 11-year-old boy named David went with his family to Williamsburg. David's family took a tour, led by a minister named Dr. William Goodwin. Dr. Goodwin explained to David's family that Williamsburg was an important part of our country's history. At Williamsburg, the first leaders of the United States, such as George Washington, Thomas Jefferson, and Patrick Henry, formed their ideas about the birth of a new nation.

During their visit, David and his family noticed that many of Williamsburg's famous buildings were rotting away. In the crumbling church, the organ was held together with shoelaces and wires. Fences sagged, and chickens ran down the muddy roads.

Dr. Goodwin hoped David's father would save Williamsburg. He wanted him to donate money to have it rebuilt and restored. After the visit, Dr. Goodwin got a telegram. It said that David's father did want to restore Williamsburg. However, he wanted his help to be a secret. For almost two years, David's father bought houses and land in Williamsburg without anyone knowing who he was. He signed telegrams "David's father."

Then, in 1928, people learned that Williamsburg's secret helper was John D. Rockefeller, Jr. He was a wealthy man who had become famous for giving gifts to help good causes. Over his lifetime, John D. Rockefeller, Jr., spent many millions of dollars to restore Williamsburg. He said his hope was that "the future may learn from the past."

At Williamsburg, actors who re-create the period dress in eighteenth-century clothing.

Rockefeller wanted to help Williamsburg because he and his son had such a great visit. "David enjoyed himself in Williamsburg," says Dennis Montgomery, a Williamsburg historian and writer. "He played with Dr. Goodwin's son, Howard. He liked the pecans that fell from the tree in Dr. Goodwin's yard. He took some home with him. He also took home some postcards and toys."

David Rockefeller still enjoys visiting Williamsburg. So do millions of tourists. The city is famous all over the world. Now people call Colonial Williamsburg "the world's largest living history museum."

Jack (left), Ben (center), and Luke Williams spent part of their school vacation visiting Williamsburg.

Recently, Jack, 11, and his brothers Ben, 9, and Luke, 5, visited Williamsburg with their family. They saw a Williamsburg very different from the one that David saw. They saw a busy town filled with actors who dressed and spoke the way people did in the 1700s. It was like stepping back in time.

"All the tour guides were dressed like eighteenth-century people," said Jack.

At the courthouse, the brothers saw men wearing waistcoats and powdered wigs and debating angrily. "They were arguing about the British taxing everybody," Jack said. "They called on people in the audience. My grandfather asked a question."

An actor demonstrates how pillories worked.

The boys watched a mock trial. To show how people were punished in the eighteenth century, the people found to be guilty were punished in front of the whole town. Their head and hands were locked in wooden frames called pillories. "People would make fun of them," said Ben.

The Williams family took a tour in a horse-drawn carriage. "The carriage ride was fun," said Ben. The boys visited the public gaol (JAYL)—the British word for jail—where some of Blackbeard's men were once held. Blackbeard was a pirate who raided ships off the North Carolina coast hundreds of years ago. "The jailkeeper was pretty cool," said Jack. "His family lived right beside the jail. The people who ran the town chose a man with a big family so they wouldn't have to pay extra for help."

The boys stopped to visit the magazine. This is where muskets and gunpowder were stored. A militia man showed the boys how citizens trained to be soldiers during the American Revolution.

"To fight in the war, a person had to be able to fire two shots in 30 seconds. That was hard because a person's musket had to be reloaded," said Ben.

"The guns were not very accurate back then," Jack added. "And they didn't shoot very far."

In the 1700s, guns were stored in magazines like this brick building.

Time Line

- **1633**—Williamsburg is founded as an outpost and called Middle Plantation
- **1699**—Williamsburg becomes capital of Virginia
- **1722**—Governor's Palace is completed
- **1754**—George Washington visits Williamsburg
- **1780**—Capital of Virginia is moved to Richmond
- **1781**—Governor's Palace burns down
- **1926**—Dr. Goodwin takes John D. Rockefeller, Jr., and his family on a tour of Williamsburg
- **1934**—Grand opening of Colonial Williamsburg. President Franklin D. Roosevelt attends
- **2001**—Colonial Williamsburg celebrates its 75th anniversary

In colonial times the Governor's Palace was one of the grandest buildings in early Williamsburg. It still is today.

The boys enjoyed visiting the Governor's Palace. The British governor had lived in this mansion before the American Revolution. During the Revolutionary War, governors of Virginia lived there. "Outside, there are statues of a lion and a unicorn, which were on the governor's coat of arms," said Jack. "In the hallways and entrance room are hundreds of guns with bayonets on the walls."

"There's a maze behind the palace," added Ben. "And a pond."

At the blacksmith's shop, the brothers saw how nails and tools were made. They learned that boys were expected to choose their trade by the age of about 10. Everywhere the brothers went in Williamsburg, they saw people who were dressed and talked as though they were from the eighteenth century.

Horses were used for working the land as well as for transportation in the 1700s and 1800s. So, the blacksmith—who made horseshoes—had an especially important job.

They even saw children who dressed in eighteenth-century styles. Annie is 11 years old and works for the Colonial Williamsburg Foundation. On the days she goes to Williamsburg, she wears a long dress, button-up shoes, and a cap called a mob cap. She has learned to use old-fashioned words such as *'tisn't* (short for *it isn't*) and *'twon't* (short for *it won't*). That helps her feel comfortable in the role she plays. It makes her fit in with the formal way people spoke 200 years ago. Annie knows how to play the spinet, an early keyboard instrument. She knows how to play eighteenth-century games such as bilbo. In bilbo, a player tosses and catches a wooden ball on a stick. Annie attended a 20-hour class to learn how to play her role.

"I really like to interact with people and talk about colonial life," Annie said. "I like wearing the costume. I like playing cricket on the palace green [lawn]."

Jack, Ben, and Luke like playing eighteenth-century games, too. The boys played a game called Huckle Buckle Beanstalk. "Someone hides a thimble anywhere in the room," Jack explains. "When you see the thimble, you yell 'Huckle Buckle Beanstalk' and sit down."

"The first person who sees the thimble gets to hide it the next time," says Ben. "The last person to see it has to do a silly thing that the others think of." Like what? "Like walking around the room and squawking like a chicken," says Jack.

The brothers visited the home of George Wythe, Thomas Jefferson's law teacher. George Wythe's signature appears on the Declaration of Independence. The Wythe House is a two-story brick house with a fireplace in each room. Fire was used for cooking, warmth, and light. People who lived in brick houses were lucky. A wooden house might burn easily, but a brick house would not. In a kitchen behind the house, Williamsburg staff members show visitors how to cook over an open fire.

This young actor is pretending to be a law student. The older actor is portraying George Wythe, a famous law teacher.

TFK FAST FACTS

- Almost half of the people living in Williamsburg at the time of the American Revolution were enslaved Africans.
- Some girls and boys were taught reading, writing, and ciphering (math). Most girls did not go to school after learning these basic skills.
- Enslaved children didn't attend school, but they were sometimes taught to read and write and do arithmetic.
- In colonial times, men wore long shirttails.
- Shoes have been found hidden inside the walls of some Williamsburg houses. No one knows why they were placed there.
- The population of Williamsburg at the time of the American Revolution was 2,000.

Meredith Poole (in pink shirt) enjoys sharing what she's learned about Williamsburg.

During their visit Jack, Ben, and Luke stopped at the site of an archaeological dig. "We saw the foundations of an old house where they were digging," said Jack. There are several active digs in Williamsburg.

Historical archaeologists focus on the time period after people started keeping written documents such as land deeds, old maps, letters, and diaries. Like detectives, archaeologists study clues to get answers to their questions. They use clues from the soil. For example, square stains in soil might mean that a posthole was dug for a fence. Archaeologists also use artifacts, or objects made by people, that they find while digging to help them learn about the past. The archaeologists are careful. They must make drawings or keep records of everything they find.

"Something is always going on in the historic area that people can watch," says Meredith Poole. She is an archaeologist. "People are surprised to find that Williamsburg still has lots of research going on. We have excavated [uncovered] only about 10 or 15 percent of the historic area. Recently we excavated a carpenter's yard. We were interested in how colonial crafts were done."

13

The archaeologists carefully clean and study what they find. First, they uncover items from recent times. As they dig deeper, they uncover older and older items. Below the items left by the early colonists, they sometimes find Native American artifacts.

"People think that archaeologists find gold pieces and jewelry and other valuable things, but that rarely happens," explains Meredith Poole. "The truth is, archaeologists mostly find things that people throw away." They find artifacts such as bricks, broken pottery, buttons, and tools.

Not many people in the eighteenth century were taught to read or write. Those who may not have learned included women, children, poor people, and enslaved Africans. These people could not leave letters, diaries, or other documents that would help archaeologists. Instead, the scientists mostly study soil and artifacts to find out more about colonial life. Archaeologists want to learn more about the daily lives of the enslaved Africans in Williamsburg. Almost half of the people living in Williamsburg at the time of the American Revolution were slaves.

Archaeologists use the clues they find to figure out what might have happened in a place. For example, suppose they are digging at a Williamsburg site. They find some marbles, an old mouth harp (harmonica), and some pieces of a porcelain doll. What could they figure out about that place? If they said that children may have lived there, they would be right.

The restoration of Colonial Williamsburg is a work in progress with new finds still being made.

In all, more than 500 buildings have been restored or reconstructed in Williamsburg. It has taken many experts and much study to rebuild this historic town. No detail is too small, from the spoons on the tables, to the pictures on the walls, to the food in the cupboards. Even the animals in Williamsburg are special. In the rare breeds program are horses, cattle, chickens, and sheep that could have been on the farms and plantations back in the 1700s.

Leicester (LES•ter) Longwool sheep were raised in Williamsburg hundreds of years ago.

Williamsburg is like a doorway to the past. More than one million visitors step through that doorway each year. Jack, Ben, and Luke learned a lot, and they also had fun. It's amazing to think how all of this has come to be. It was all a result of a caring minister taking "David's father" on a tour of Williamsburg almost 80 years ago.

TFK 5

TOP 5 SIGHTS IN WILLIAMSBURG
1. Governor's Palace
2. the Capitol
3. the Magazine
4. Peyton Randolph House
5. George Wythe House

This actor's portrayal of Thomas Jefferson is one of many things that attract so many visitors to Williamsburg every year.